# Godly Moms

**Strength from the Inside Out**

To our daughters, Bev, Donna, Robbie, and Janet, the joy of my heart. Without you I wouldn't have a word to say.

And to my husband, Bob, the love of my life, for all the ways you lift my heart.

I thank God for any wisdom in my words. It came through the gentle teaching of the Spirit of Christ.

# Godly Moms

## Strength from the Inside Out

Lenore Buth

CONCORDIA PUBLISHING HOUSE · SAINT LOUIS

Published by Concordia Publishing House
3558 S. Jefferson Avenue, St. Louis, MO 63118-3968
1-800-325-3040 • www.cph.org

All rights reserved. No part of this publication may be reproduced, stored in a retrieval system, or transmitted, in any form or by any means, electronic, mechanical, photocopying, recording, or otherwise, without the prior written permission of Concordia Publishing House.

Text copyright © 2013 Lenore Buth

Scripture quotations unless otherwise noted are from the ESV Bible® (The Holy Bible, English Standard Version®), copyright © 2001 by Crossway Bibles, a publishing ministry of Good News Publishers. Used by permission. All rights reserved.

Scripture quotations marked NKJV™ are taken from the New King James Version®. Copyright © 1982 by Thomas Nelson, Inc. Used by permission. All rights reserved.

Cover art © Shutterstock, Inc.

Manufactured in the United States of America

2 3 4 5 6 7 8 9 10     22 21 20 19 18 17 16 15 14

Presentation

for:

from:

# Table of Contents

| | |
|---|---|
| Introduction: From Lenore, with Love | 8 |
| Made for Each Other | 12 |
| Be a Mom like Harold Hill | 14 |
| Abandon the Struggle to Know It All | 16 |
| Seeing Past That Strong Will | 18 |
| Over in the Blink of an Eye | 20 |
| Safeguard Yourself and Your Marriage | 22 |
| A Gleam of Light for Dark Days | 24 |
| If You're Rearing Your Children on Your Own | 26 |
| Kids Will Be Kids | 28 |
| Know the Value of Your Life | 30 |
| What to Do with Fantasy Dads | 32 |
| Who Needs Whom? | 34 |
| He Never Promised You a Rose Garden | 36 |
| One Day at a Time | 38 |
| Look beyond Frustration with Your Difficult Child | 40 |
| Beware the Greenhouse Effect | 42 |
| Never Enough of Me | 44 |
| Limits Testing | 46 |
| Don't Just Do Something—Stand There | 48 |
| Among the Missing: You | 50 |
| Checked Your Glasses Lately? | 52 |

| | |
|---|---|
| Factor in Faith | 54 |
| Be Careful Where You Look | 56 |
| Forget Yesterday—Look at Who You Are Today | 58 |
| Avoid Hanging Verbal Weights on Your Child | 60 |
| Present a United Front | 62 |
| Mom, the Chief Nurturer | 64 |
| Move from Conflict to Strength | 66 |
| So What Am I, Chopped Liver? | 68 |
| Living with Uncertainty | 70 |
| Mealtimes Nourish Family Bonds | 72 |
| Are Your Kids Training You to Obey? | 74 |
| Making Sense of the Struggle and Finding Hope | 76 |
| Resistance Comes in Different Packages | 78 |
| Take It Easier | 80 |
| Why Bother Going to Church? | 82 |
| Mom, the Balance Beam Pro | 84 |
| Don't Wait Too Long to Talk about Sex | 86 |
| Never Underestimate Dear Old Dad | 88 |
| Failure Rates a Passing Grade | 90 |
| Mothering: Stretching beyond Yourself | 92 |
| The Child in Your Mind May Not Be the Child in Your Life | 94 |
| Your Pedestal Is Crumbling, But That's Okay | 96 |
| Pause and Be Refreshed | 98 |
| A Woman of Lasting Influence | 100 |

# From Lenore, with Love

Dear Mom,

Think of this little book as a warm hug from a friend.

It's about deepening your inner strength and helping your kids develop theirs.

I've walked in your shoes. I know that feeling of being overwhelmed, always tired to the bone, and aching for an encouraging word. My continual prayer was "Lord JESUS, help me, please!"

Before I became a mom, I thought, how hard can it be?

Afterward, I knew.

This is the book I longed for then, but never found. Like you, I wondered how to sort out wisdom from passing theories. I wanted our girls to grow up with a solid foundation of faith and sound values. Close behind were confidence and common sense.

But how to do it?

One day an older friend stated her guiding principle for parenting: "A mother's job is to work herself out of a job long before her children leave home."

My jaw dropped. Did she mean that the way it sounded?

Yes. She went on to explain that it means letting youngsters assume an ever-increasing responsibility for themselves. Allowing them to discover that choices bring consequences. As they acquire self-discipline, their can-do attitude grows. In effect, our children are ready to live on their own before they leave home.

Naturally, Mom feels less stressed and harried. As she watches her kids cope with daily life, she feels joy and satisfaction.

When they fail—and they will—this mom picks them up, doles out hugs, and nudges them to try again.

They grow stronger.

Their healthy self-image is based on proof, not praise.

Jesus told us to love our neighbors as ourselves, and our children qualify as "close neighbors." We love them most truly when we help them become stronger from the inside out, when we teach them from the start that our value comes because there is One who loves us perfectly despite ourselves. They grow up to be balanced young adults, ready for life. That's our gift to them.

And to ourselves.

This is not a book of techniques but rather principles. It's as much about you as your children. I want you to know that nothing else in life carries the same lasting significance.

I pray that my simple sharing will be a blessing to you.

Oh, one thing more. God made you a mom. He will supply the wisdom and strength you need for each day.

You see, I can say this because I lived it and know it to be true.

With love,<br>
Lenore

# Made for Each Other

Your family is no accident. God gave you to each other.

Each child who calls you "Mom" was created just for you.

God placed you together because you need each other.

Let those sentences sink deep into your heart and your mind.

This is true even when you have conflicts and difficulties. Even if you are as different as plums and peanut butter. Even though it seems you always say or do the wrong thing with one of your children.

Your Designer Kids need *you*, not the Ms. Flawless Mom who lives on the corner.

And vice versa.

You don't need the placid child next door, nor Super Kid across the street. You need that one who most often baffles you or challenges you.

God tailor-makes our children to stretch us.

To teach us.

To grow us.

Mothering opens our minds and strips away old, comfortable illusions about life.

And about ourselves.

Day after day, we're forced to cope. As we do, we may discover strengths we didn't know we had.

Weaknesses too.

No mom would label this process easy or comfortable. Growing pains never are.

When you feel overwhelmed, reassure yourself with what you know. God put together the pieces of your family jigsaw puzzle according to His plan.

It is a good one.

So walk on, trust Jesus, and be at peace.

Like your kids, you're in the process of becoming. Your heart will never shrink back to its original size.

---

> [The Lord says,] "Before I formed you in the womb I knew you." Jeremiah 1:5a

## P.S.

Ignore those stretch marks on your tummy. What counts are the stretch marks on your heart and mind and spirit. New ones will keep showing up over the years—and that's a good thing.

# Be a Mom like Harold Hill

Maybe you remember Professor Harold Hill from *The Music Man*.

This fellow could talk, and he drilled confidence into his "players." They would be wonderful, he said. If they only believed, they would out-perform every other band. Finally the rag-tag group held real instruments. To everyone's amazement (including the professor's), they played a halting version of *Minuet in G*.

Call it Exhibit A in helping each youngster "fake it 'til you make it."

We moms possess far greater power than Harold Hill did.

Our children naturally believe our words. When we express our confidence, they gain courage, even when they pretend to be too cool to care.

You may say, "I know you can do it," and hear, "Well, you're my mother. You're supposed to say that."

Pay attention, however, and you'll notice your son or daughter stands a bit taller. Knowing their parents believe in them helps kids do better and tune out the pint-size critics around them.

Kids listen especially well to your casual, not-meant-for-them-to-hear remarks, so watch your words. As a mom, every word you say is worth its weight in rubies.

Or rocks.

Even Professor Harold Hill couldn't make that claim.

---

> Let no corrupting talk come out of your mouths, but only such as is good for building up, . . . that it may give grace to those who hear. Ephesians 4:29

P.S.

Ask God what "Harold Hill" words each one needs to hear, then specialize in speaking rubies.

# Abandon the Struggle to Know It All

Some moms live in Tension City and they're proud of it.

They devour guidebooks on child development at different ages and stages. They track their children's progress, constantly wondering whether their kids measure up.

Who wouldn't be uptight?

Rearing a child bears no resemblance to conducting a science experiment. Step A does not necessarily lead to Step B. Research studies abound, each one citing endless statistics and averages. Yet even world-famous experts can only guess about any individual.

Every child is a one-time creation.

Unpredictable.

Full of potential we cannot glimpse.

Remember that.

Otherwise, you may slot your son or daughter into a category, then adjust your perception and expectations to fit. Or you might compare your child using timetables written by "the experts" instead of your eyes and ears.

When you do that, you cheat your kids.

Rearing our children remains one of the great adventures in life. No doubt God planned it that way. Otherwise, how would we moms grow? Why would we pray? Only the Creator can say what is within each child. He knows us too, and He promises to supply what we need when we need it. Jesus died and rose again. He frees us from fear, and we can live fully.

So give up trying to have all the answers, and enjoy the surprises.

Besides, anxiety brings on early wrinkles.

---

> Great is our Lord, and abundant in power; His understanding is beyond measure. The LORD lifts up the humble.
> Psalm 147:5–6a

## P.S.

Sometimes what we think we know for sure isn't quite accurate. Pray for fresh insight into each child and a sensitive heart.

# Seeing Past That Strong Will

Some of us moms have kids who came out stubborn. The never-ending battle of wills leaves us limp.

You look at your junior-grade freedom fighter and sigh.

Must everything be a battle?

Suppose you did a 180. A shift in viewpoint. Decide to look past your frustration and this child's balkiness. Choose to fasten on strengths.

That breathtaking force of will? This kid goes after what he wants. Those everlasting comebacks? She can argue any point with convincing logic. That maddening refusal to give in? Difficulties will never faze this one. He will finish what he starts.

Your child's temperament is no accident. Psalm 139 says God created your son or daughter.

On purpose.

For a purpose.

Your mission is to temper that iron-rod will, not break it.

Maybe your kid seems proud of being known as "the problem child." He or she may wear that badge as a cover-up for being lonely and feeling out of sync in your family.

Lonely is what we feel when we don't fit in.

Love is what we long for.

Jesus can give you fresh love for this youngster, love wiped clean of painful memories.

Fix your gaze on the One who makes all things new.

Even your tired heart.

Even your child's stubborn will.

---

> Therefore, if anyone is in Christ, he is a new creation. The old has passed away; behold, the new has come.
> 2 Corinthians 5:17

## P.S.

Ask God for eyes that see and a spirit willing to let Christ's love flow through you.

# Over in the Blink of an Eye

Look out for when/then thinking.

Every mom has spoken her own version of this script.

You know the lines. "Once she's out of preschool, I'll have my days to myself."

"Little League practice and games can't end soon enough for me. I am really tired of sitting on those bleachers for hours and waiting around when practice runs late."

"I can't wait for her to get her driver's license. Then she can chauffeur herself to school and those endless after-school activities. I will be so glad!"

How many times have you started a sentence with "It will be wonderful when . . ."?

With eyes intently fastened on the next "when," you might forget to notice the here and now.

Truth is, here and now is all you've got.

Soon enough, children fly away.

Soon enough, you'll be done.

That's when you will see clearly the meaning, the poignant sweetness of today. Of family, all together in one place.

You will comprehend the joy of today's jam-packed existence.

You will ache to relive even twenty-four hours of this present time.

Only you won't be able to.

Nobody can.

So breathe deep and savor this moment. Treasure this ordinary, extraordinary day.

It is the gift of God.

Besides, it's the only one fit to live in.

---

> This is the day that the LORD has made;
> let us rejoice and be glad in it.
> Psalm 118:24

## P.S.

Be present in your life now, while you're living it, before it morphs into a memory.

# Safeguard Yourself and Your Marriage

Being a mom, keeping up with everything, can consume us. Sometimes we feel hollow, as if we drained our physical and emotional energy accounts.

Lately you go through your days mindlessly. Walking around, but dead inside. Nothing in life brings you joy—not even your marriage.

Call a halt.

Now.

Make time to be alone and pour out your hurt at the cross. Jesus experienced every human emotion, so He understands. You can trust Him to hear and to answer as He knows best.

Why stop there? Read a while in the Bible, perhaps the Psalms or the Gospel of John. Some verses will seem written just for you, so mark them and "chew on them" through the day. Think of this as a sort of oasis in your day when you take in living water so you don't run dry.

Promise yourself never to get caught in this trap again. Otherwise your children will live with an empty shell that only looks and sounds like you.

So will your husband.

By the way, watch that your marriage relationship doesn't become an afterthought. Taking time for each other does not rob your kids. Rather, you bless them. Children who are confident that their mom and dad love each other feel more secure.

Shoehorn daily time for just the two of you into your crazy schedules. Even fifteen minutes a day can help you stay connected.

Nurturing your marriage and your faith life is a necessity, not an indulgence.

You're a mom, so you constantly give of yourself to those you love.

Keep the reservoir of your heart overflowing. Then you naturally will splash out love and blessings on your family.

> And may the Lord make you increase and abound in love for one another and for all, as we do for you.
> 1 Thessalonians 3:12

## P.S.

Common sense says you don't have time for all this. Wisdom says you can't afford not to.

# A Gleam of Light
## for Dark Days

At times life bursts with joy that warms us and plants an inner smile that won't quit. We bask in the glow as long as we can, always wishing it could last.

Other days feel heavy, like a mantle of fog that refuses to budge. Usually the mood passes before long and we come back into the sunlight.

Not always.

Sometimes we get stuck in it, bogged down by problems or by our lack of power. It seems all we can do is watch and wait and pray.

Maybe that's where you are this minute, feeling exhausted and at the end of your endurance.

Sometimes you think you cannot go on.

Reason nags, "There is no hope."

Logic asks, "Why bother?"

Faith shouts something quite different: "You are not alone!" Sure, it defies human reason to believe Jesus is all sufficient in every circumstance. That's the point. To believe means to trust what cannot be explained. The One who said "Lo, I am with you always" walks with you every day, through every challenge.

He will light your way for each next step and be your strength.

Rest in His promise.

He is bigger than whatever you face. (Remember Good Friday? and Easter?)

Etch His words on the tablets of your despair, and be at peace.

> "I am the Lord, the God of all flesh. Is anything too hard for Me?" Jeremiah 32:27

## P.S.

Pray for a mind and spirit willing to let go of your gloom and be made new by God's grace in Jesus Christ.

# If You're Rearing Your Children on Your Own

All responsibility for parenting your kids rests on your weary shoulders.

No backup.

No breaks.

No one to talk things over with.

Child support may be iffy or nonexistent. You barely manage the basics, yet you long to give your children "the advantages."

Look deeper. Your kids already possess treasure. You.

They know they can count on you. They have your love, your acceptance, your faith in them. You listen with your heart and hug away their pain on bad days. Be sure they know what your faith means to you.

On the job.

In your mothering.

In times of discouragement.

Never fear your struggles and failures might cancel out your witness. Rather, your kids will know real faith endures in real life.

That's a powerful backup for what they learn when they go along to church and Sunday School. There they interact with believers of all ages and make friends. Each week they hear again that they belong to Jesus, that He loves them and is with them every day.

Your children are growing up rich.

Believe it.

Emphasize teamwork. Assign regular chores, and monitor performance. You'll hear complaints, but never mind. They are practicing life.

Building confidence.

Growing stronger.

Give up fretting about counterfeits like the "best" schools, the "right" clothes. You already provide them the real thing.

Yes, you're a single parent. You also are a blessing to your children.

Let that balm your heart and give you peace.

---

Not that we are sufficient in ourselves
to claim anything as coming from us,
but our sufficiency is from God.
2 Corinthians 3:5

## P.S.

Trust that every day, your loving Savior walks beside you and His love is with you. He knows the way and will not let you fall.

# Kids Will Be Kids

Your youngster flooded the dinner table with milk.

Again.

Implored you to find a restroom ten minutes after you left home.

Again.

Woke the baby from her nap, this time by practicing Tarzan yells in the hall.

How did you react?

Some moms routinely explode when their kids are messy.

Forgetful.

Noisy.

Other moms remain unruffled, insisting that culprits help with damage control.

Most probably do some of each. How you react matters because you're the family thermostat. You set the emotional climate at your house.

For everyone.

Take another look.

For starters, consider your child's age. A six-year-old is not a twelve-year-old.

Evaluate the evidence. Was this willful disobedience? or normal "kid stuff"?

The first can't be ignored.

The second may call for little more than understanding and benign neglect.

You will have days when you can't handle one more thing. That's your signal it's time to stretch again. Time to call for Help beyond yourself. Time to pray for balance, a calm spirit, and a daily supply of fresh love for each child. Time to receive Christ's mercy.

Give yourself some leeway as you grow—and give some to your kids too. Mothering continually bumps us up against one inescapable truth:

Children tend to be, well, childish.

They can't be anything else.

---

When I was a child, I spoke like a child, I thought like a child, I reasoned like a child. 1 Corinthians 13:11a

## P.S.

Kids tend to mess up adult schedules and inconvenience their parents, then get scolded for misbehaving. They think that's unfair. What do you think?

# Know the Value of Your Life

It is your season of mothering.

Time for yourself: only a memory.

Energy: never enough; you live on perpetual overload.

Sometimes you question whether you are "accomplishing anything" with your life. On your worst days, you wonder whether any of it matters to anyone.

So hear it again and forever: yes, it does.

No spreadsheets will track the worth of your days. No pay raises for working your way up the corporate ladder or bonuses for good performance. No extended vacation time for years of service.

Yet, each day counts, even the ones that feel like a washout. Their value lies in this: you are there.

Laughing.

Reminding.

Hugging.

Cleaning up after.

Soothing away fears.

Giving pep talks.

Modeling for your kids in a thousand ways what love means. Teaching them in real time that love makes up for a multitude of shortcomings. Yours and theirs.

For now, give up looking for lasting proof of your effectiveness. It's too soon.

Consider rearing your children an act of faith. It is.

Trust Jesus to be your strength in every circumstance. He will.

He who is love walks beside you, through every today and every tomorrow.

---

> For everything there is a season, and a time for every matter under heaven.
> Ecclesiastes 3:1

P.S.

Even as your children grow visibly taller, you grow deeper and more well grounded, all unseen. Count on it.

# What to Do with Fantasy Dads

Dads come in all shapes, sizes, and personalities.

Sometimes we moms forget and latch onto a glorified image of what the father of our children *ought* to be. We look at photos of celebrity dads cradling their little ones or romping in the park (with nannies waiting). We think, *Oh, isn't that beautiful?* Before we know it, we're into the muck: *If only my husband were like that. If only he cared that much.*

Time for a reality check.

The perfect earthly father exists only in print and on-screen.

Some days, real-life fathers wake up tired. They want to roll over in bed and be left alone. Some days they want to skip going to work and go play.

Even a dad who loves his wife and kids sometimes feels overwhelmed by responsibility that stretches ahead for years. He harbors private dreams too.

Yet he stays.

In today's society, that constitutes a marvel. A busy mom can take this wonder for granted. A faithful dad whose word can be trusted gives his children a lifetime gift simply by being there.

Day after day.

Through good times and bad.

Living out love in tangible ways.

A real-life dad who loves, who tries, who stays trumps any fantasy dad on the planet.

If this dad believes in Jesus as his Lord and Savior, then his children are doubly blessed.

---

> Let us run with endurance the race that is set before us, looking to Jesus, the founder and perfecter of our faith.
> Hebrews 12:1b–2a

## P.S.

Rock hunters sometimes discover that what appears plain and boring can hide treasure inside. So do wives.

# Who Needs Whom?

What signals mother love for you?

A lot of moms think loving means giving.

"Here, let me do that for you, sweetie."

"You want it right now? Of course, darling."

"You promised to make those decorations by tomorrow? But it's your bedtime. Okay, one more time, I will make them for you."

Maybe you know this woman. She pours breakfast cereal and fixes school lunches. She locates the lost hairbrush, windbreaker, or backpack. She makes sure homework gets done and gathers up school papers. She rounds up uniforms and equipment, snacks and water bottles. Instead of complaining, this mother rejoices: she is needed.

All the time.

By everybody.

Before awarding a medal for selflessness, weigh another possibility. Caring for a "helpless" family sometimes provides an excuse to dodge other issues and other needs. What looks like "giving-ness" may in fact be "keeping-ness."

To love by keeping our family dependent can be a subtle way of maintaining control. After a while they will be unable to function without us.

And we without them.

This strategy will never build inner strength.

Not in children.
Not in moms.

Avoid this trap by being clear on your goals for your kids and for yourself. Keeping the balance can be tricky, but it's vital.

After all, no kid can fly solo while holding on tightly to Mommy's hand.

---

> Little children, let us not love in word or talk but in deed and in truth.
> 1 John 3:18

## P.S.

Let your question be, *What builds strength in my children?* Your answer will show you how to love them wisely.

# He Never Promised You a Rose Garden

Sometimes all that keeps us going is commitment.

Faithfulness to vows made before we understood what we were promising.

Dedication to rearing our children.

All of it more than we bargained for, both the wonder and the woe.

Today you stay because you pledged you would. You try not to ask yourself, *Is this all there is?*

Maybe so, for right now.

Life can be like that sometimes, even in the best marriages, the happiest families. Even for Christians.

Plant another truth down deep: perfection never will be found, not in your husband or any other human being.

Not in your children.

Not in yourself.

If you keep expecting it, you set yourself up to be frustrated and discontented.

Rest your heart on this: Like the sun behind a cloudy day, the Lord's faithful presence and love remain with you. The One who pledged to bring light from darkness, who gave you His perfect love, will work all things for good in His time.

He assures you of strength for your journey, but never a flawless life. You can count on Him to fuel your resolve and provide staying power one day after another.

Until love returns and joy floods your heart once more.

Until you want to be a wife and a mom.

All over again.

---

> Why are you cast down, O my soul, and why are you in turmoil within me? Hope in God; for I shall again praise Him, my salvation and my God.
> Psalm 42:11

## P.S.

During winter's bleak days, a plant may look dead, but its roots live on. God always brings another spring.

# One Day at a Time

Sometimes all that keeps us going is knowing what we do matters.

Take all that "mom stuff" you could live without, like cleaning up after two kids with stomach flu while feeling queasy yourself.

Melted crayons in the clothes dryer.

Goldfish floating in fish bowls and hamsters hiding behind the washer.

Smelly socks under couches and milk congealing in glasses on windowsills.

For your child's sake, you do what it takes.

Endure another piano recital, waiting to clap and praying she gets through her piece.

Huddle under an old blanket at a frigid Little League game, ready to cheer if your kid gets a turn at bat.

Tie on a ridiculous party hat just to see your child grin.

Some days you think you have nothing left to give. But you keep giving, willing to spend yourself for your family, the people you love most in this world. Believing your purpose from God stretches way beyond this day.

You know the "why" of your life so you can handle the "how"—looking at your kids, hearing their irrepressible laughter energize your spirit.

So you breathe deep, pray once more for strength, and smile.
Ready to lay down your life all over again.

> [Jesus said,] "As the Father has loved Me, so have I loved you. Abide in My love. . . . Greater love has no one than this, that someone lay down his life for his friends." John 15:9,13

## P.S.

Even your most trying days are the stuff of tomorrow's "good old days." Pray for a heart that sees this now, while you're in the midst, so you can laugh today instead of tomorrow.

# Look beyond Frustration with Your Difficult Child

Some of us live with a kid who tests our endurance.

Endlessly.

We question our ability to go on.

Often.

Let the child who drives you to distraction drive you back to God. He gave you this one too, and He never makes a mistake. Pray for His wisdom and patience so you can live out love, even on not-so-good days.

When you feel drained, rely on His strength to carry you through.

When you fail, give it to Christ, cling to His grace, and begin again.

Watch your word choices because whatever you speak aloud magnifies what is—or isn't. Be generous with encouragement, even for attempts to do right, and be stingy with pointing out faults.

You can cut down on battles between you if you stay consistent and stick with limits you set.

Wrap everything you do and say in love.

Even if.

Even when.

Even though.

Don't give in—and don't give up on this kid.

You cannot peek through a knothole in tomorrow's fence. Your same challenging child may mature into an outstanding adult.

Picture that inventive mind wisely used, that strong will harnessed for good. Through the Spirit of Jesus working within, that's not a foolish dream. Then your heart will overflow with thanks and pride and joy.

Meanwhile, hang on.

Be patient.

Trust.

You have all you need to live this day.

Every day.

---

> And this is the confidence that we have toward Him, that if we ask anything according to His will He hears us.
> 1 John 5:14

## P.S.

This young gift of God is helping you grow—whether you want to or not. And didn't you always say you wanted to?

# Beware the Greenhouse Effect

Overprotected kids are like hothouse plants: unless pampered, they wilt.

We all know loving moms who shelter their kids from life. Predictably, their children always expect to be rescued.

Easily take offense.

Complain, loudly and often.

Such youngsters seldom delight anyone, even themselves.

Children who learn to deal with absolutes grow up advantaged. Every school day guarantees opportunities to learn that life is not fair.

Yes, some people do squeak by on charm.

Natural talents and intelligence do vary.

Friends they counted on may let them down.

These are hard facts of life at any age, but only kids permitted to struggle with reality nail these lessons. To always shield your children from truth will stunt their emotional development.

Protect them from violence and abuse, yes. Otherwise, skip the salvage operation unless somebody's drowning.

Allow your youngsters to cope.

And learn.

Keep hugs and encouragement coming as you listen and talk things through. Gently offer advice and suggestions if you're asked.

Be their guide, not their personal 911 service.

Then your son or daughter can grow strong enough to survive without your at-the-elbow watchfulness. Most of all, pray that the Spirit of Christ will work a teachable heart within each youngster. Over time, every challenge your child faces will deposit wisdom, build character, and develop confidence. Think of it as readying your son or daughter for life. Your kids will leave home already "toughened up" so they can thrive on their own.

Just like young plants.

---

> But let patience have its perfect work, that you may be perfect and complete, lacking nothing. James 1:4 (NKJV)

## P.S.

Often the kindest—and hardest—thing you can do for your child is back off.

# Never Enough of Me

Moms don't do spare time, not in the real world.

Mostly we muddle through, trying to be all things to all people, all the time. The mythical Perfect Mother teases from just ahead, and we never quite catch up. Watching her makes us want to quit.

You can stop doubting yourself if you fix your thoughts on what the Bible says.

Psalm 139 says God created you and each of your children.

He saw you before you were born.

He knows your thoughts and your words before you speak them.

He watches over you in all your ways, all your days.

This you can rely on.

He put your family together, whether your children were planned, unplanned, or came by adoption or by marriage.

Sometimes all you can offer is your weary self and your love that won't quit. That is sufficient.

Christ's strength will carry you through.

He can work all things for good, even your weaknesses.

Jesus is hope in discouragement, joy in despair, peace in the midst of pressure.

Commit yourself and your family to His loving care. Know that you are living out His purpose for you.

Growing.
Trusting.
Walking by faith, one day at a time.
It will be more than enough.

---

> [Jesus said,] "I am the vine; you are the branches. Whoever abides in Me and I in him, he it is that bears much fruit, for apart from Me you can do nothing." John 15:5

## P.S.

God never gives you more than twenty-four hours in your day, but He can stretch your time. Try asking Him.

# Limits Testing

Few of us moms live the life we imagined. In that beautiful world, we would be so loving, so sweet and joyful every moment.

In this here-and-now world, sometimes you burst with love. Other times you operate on empty. You can feel so connected to your child, it's as if you were two halves of a whole.

Or so distant that you could hail from different planets.

You are the hub—and the heart—of your family. Most of the time you wouldn't trade being a mom for all the gold in Russian vaults.

Today, however, you've had it.

Every mom alive reaches this point at some point. Yet, all that changes from one time to another is perspective. Once you put on your dark glasses, everything looks dark.

Shed those shades and take another look at your life in the light.

Remember who you are. And whose you are.

The God who made you a mom also outfitted you with everything you require on your trek through mothering. Whatever situation this day may bring, you already possess every quality you will need to handle it. Whatever the challenge, you are up to it.

You *can* cope.

Tomorrow's demands never can outstrip tomorrow's supply of energy and strength, so relax.

Trust.

Persevere.

The One who designed you—and each of your children—knows your limits.

---

> For we are His workmanship, created in Christ Jesus for good works, which God prepared beforehand, that we should walk in them. Ephesians 2:10

## P.S.

If you question how your personality and character traits fit you to be a mother to your kids, don't worry. *He* knows.

# Don't Just Do Something—Stand There

It happens in the best of families.

Kids poke and tease and argue, especially when they live under the same roof.

Some moms seek to arbitrate never-ending tussles over playthings, cell phones, and whose turn it is to feed the cat. We feel important and needed, but there's a downside.

When our sons and daughters run to us with every grievance, they never learn to work things out on their own.

Choose a better way—let them work it out. As they do, they develop negotiating skills and gain inner strength. Maintain a listening ear and an open mind, always alert for undercurrents.

Perhaps, as reported, the bigger kid bullied the smaller one again for no reason. Or maybe that sweet little sister or brother is an artful puppet master.

Intervene if someone is bleeding, of course. Separate the foes, treat the boo-boos, and deliver Lecture No. 3,147. Sometimes that will be enough.

One more time, go over what's acceptable in your family, then insist they repeat it back to you.

Now walk away.

Let these pint-size opponents negotiate their own peace settlement. And grow.

Consider each squabble a class project, as if you were teaching a course called "Mastering Interpersonal Skills 101."

Because you are.

And as you teach, you also grow.

---

Fulfill my joy by being like-minded, having the same love, being of one accord, of one mind. Philippians 2:2 (NKJV)

## P.S.

Pray for insight and discernment to know when to jump in and when to hold back. Then trust Jesus Christ and relax. You'll know what to do.

# Among the Missing: You

Nobody told you it would be easy.

Nobody told you it would be this hard.

You love your husband, and you'd throw yourself in front of a truck for your kids. But you feel buried.

Weary of being needed.

When do you get to put yourself first?

Ask any mom. The mood sneaks up on you, as deadly as quicksand.

Avoid slipping into self-pity.

Grab hold of the Rescuer who won't let you sink, and talk with Him, heart to heart. Spend some time reading His Word. Receive His living refreshment.

Now take another look at pluses and minuses in your life. Name the people who stand out and those who nurture you with their love and encouragement. Take a reading of your strengths and flaws.

Give thanks for what is and let what isn't fade away.

Don't be dismayed if you start sliding again. Nobody grows in a straight line. Just pause and re-inventory your life.

All of it.

That inner wail may start up again, with its too-familiar lyrics: "When will it be my turn?" Be ready with your new refrain and answer back: "Sooner than I can imagine."

Here's the stunner: it will seem no longer than an eyeblink before you look back on these days with twinges of longing.

You'll even wonder how you missed so much joy.

Don't.

Rather, pray for fresh eyes to see.

---

> Fear not, for I am with you; be not dismayed, for I am your God; I will strengthen you, I will help you, I will uphold you with My righteous right hand. Isaiah 41:10

## P.S.

Ask God to tune your heart to hear the joyful melody of your life.

# Checked Your Glasses Lately?

Every mom has muttered to herself, "There should be more to life than this."

Personality clashes that wear us out.

Annoying habits that frustrate.

Failings that mock us because nothing changes.

Ever since Eden, that's all there is.

In our husbands.

In our children.

In ourselves.

That's life among us sinners. Even sinners redeemed and loved by Jesus.

We remain distressingly—and wondrously—human, endowed with the God-given capacity to choose our outlook on life.

You can rail against your life and the people in it—or rejoice in the good. Point out what's missing—or applaud what's there. Complain about the thorns—or revel in the rose blossoms.

Every moment of every day, in every situation, you choose where you look.

Will you stare at the mud—or marvel at the stars?

Your copycat kids watch and listen, soaking up cues on how to live from their hero.

You.

Your view of life will become theirs.

Ready for a new perspective?

Trust the One who gave sight to the blind.

Let Him open the eyes of your heart to the good in your life and the people in it.

Then get ready to rejoice and give thanks.

> The LORD is my strength and my shield; in Him my heart trusts, and I am helped; my heart exults, and with my song I give thanks to Him. Psalm 28:7

## P.S.

Concentrating on the negative is like wearing blinders and thinking you see all that's there.

# Factor in Faith

Some loving moms (and dads) think the Bible amounts to a bunch of old, outdated rules or a bunch of beliefs they can pick and choose from. They would not impose such "shackles" on their innocent children. "Let them decide once they reach adulthood."

"Besides," they ask, "how is God relevant to a modern child?"

Other parents wrap their lives around a solid core of faith that spills over to their children.

Weigh the evidence.

Kids who believe God watches over them find the world less scary.

Lonely youngsters who know "Jesus loves me" snuggle into a Comforter they carry with them.

Children who struggle and mess up and fail understand that they always measure up because of Jesus and His cross.

They can read it themselves in the Bible in verses like John 3:16.

Kids who trust there's a divine purpose for their lives will not be so overwhelmed by disappointments and frustrations.

Young believers usually choose friends based on more than appearance and popularity. They find the blueprint for healthy relationships in Christ's brief command, "Love your neighbor as yourself."

Christian young people measure by a constant reference point beyond their own experience, emotions, and peer groups.

Faith in God is the inner compass by which they steer—the plumb line by which to distinguish the crooked line from the straight.

Judge for yourself. Are kids who grow up believing in Jesus victimized?

Or blessed?

---

> In the fear of the LORD one has strong confidence, and His children will have a refuge. Proverbs 14:26

## P.S.

When you plant faith and Bible teachings in your children's hearts, you give them a gift that stays with them for life.

# Be Careful Where You Look

Right from the beginning, life turned inside out.

Every mom knows that instant flash of recognition. At once, our child owns us—heart, mind, and body.

Some days we feel swallowed up by motherhood.

Sometimes we ache for what we've lost. That pre-baby figure, for instance, the one with the tiny waistline. Uninterrupted sleep and private time. Quiet dinners, with adult conversation.

Warning: Hazardous thinking zone ahead. Proceed with caution. Self-pity waits to move in and set up housekeeping, with bitterness close behind.

Is that how you want to live?

Turn away. Focus on what you gained, like your child's sunshine smile.

Purpose in your days, no matter what else is or isn't going on.

Meaning for your existence.

A deeper understanding of love.

A reason to keep going that keeps you going.

Count on everyday irritations, as predictable as weeds in a garden.

Joy lives at your house too, waiting to be noticed. Are you looking for it? You will find it if you live this moment fully and embrace your life now. Reflect on the wonder: God entrusted you with your child's life and love. God made you His children through Jesus.

Let that fill your heart with gladness.

Moments strung together make a life.

You alone dictate the colors of the beads.

---

> But the righteous shall be glad; they shall exult before God; they shall be jubilant with joy! Psalm 68:3

P.S.

Ask God to make you a joy spotter.

# Forget Yesterday—Look at Who You Are Today

Perhaps you lacked advantages or grew up in a troubled family.

Maybe you've logged your own share of mistakes.

You learned, sometimes the hard way.

You grew, not always the best way.

You left your past behind, but not your self-doubt.

Sometimes you wake in the night and a question yammers at you: *With my background, what do I have to offer my children?* Start with a love so strong you would give your life for them.

Faith in Jesus as your Savior, for another.

Principles you now know are right and good.

Authenticity that comes through when you speak with your kids about dangers that lurk and making mistakes.

Feed your spirit. Join a Bible study or small group at your church. You'll meet other moms and make new friends.

Never think yourself limited by your past. The One who rose from the tomb can make you new by His Spirit.

Whenever the past weighs you down again, give Him the load again. Repeat as needed until you feel the freedom you already possess in Christ.

**Every morning is a fresh start.**

Ask God to enable you to dwell fully in this life you're living.

You owe it to your kids.

You owe it to yourself.

---

> There is therefore now no condemnation for those who are in Christ Jesus. For the law of the Spirit of life has set you free in Christ Jesus from the law of sin and death. Romans 8:1–2

P.S.

**You can be free of the past only if you are willing to let go of it.**

# Avoid Hanging Verbal Weights on Your Child

Many adults still wear hidden nametags they've hated since childhood, more inescapable than tattoos. Some thoughtless early remark(s) became their self-identity.

We all know our own.

Every mom has spoken without thinking and later wished she could take back the words.

Remarks like "I guess she's a klutz like me."

Or "He's always been slow in school."

"She's a bit chunky; baby fat, I hope."

"He's driving me crazy! He's so hyper, just like my brother."

Et cetera.

The problem is, kids believe their parents' words and lodge them deep within.

These mind tags become an excuse.

Or a millstone.

Perhaps right now you remembered something you said. Don't let it go. Find a quiet place to be alone with your child. Humbly confess and ask forgiveness. Pray together that God will melt away old hurts and memories.

Your words count more than you know.

How your kids see themselves starts with what they hear from you. Plant the certainty that each child is God's one-of-a-kind creation and made a unique purpose, that each child is loved by a saved by Christ Jesus. Paint these growing-up years as a time to discover who they are, and reassure your kids that your love for them will never waver, even when they struggle.

Never mind if they seem to pooh-pooh your words.

The ears of their hearts remain wide open, ready to take in and record every word you say.

For life.

---

Set a guard, O LORD, over my mouth; keep watch over the door of my lips!
Psalm 141:3

## P.S.

Pray for insight. Make affirming each child's strengths your new habit.

# Present a United Front

Family patterns can develop before we're even aware of them.

Maybe one parent usually says no, while the other says yes.

Guess which one their children go to first.

Kids also know which topics are a surefire yes with one parent and a no-no with the other.

The younger generation easily gains proficiency in manipulation and negotiation.

Your best strategy is to eliminate any reward for playing one parent against the other. Remember who you are. God puts parents in charge of their children. That means you and your husband work out basic family guidelines when you're alone together, separate from family meetings where children vote and make suggestions.

Decide together what is and is not allowed.

Promise to always talk over a child's request together and to discuss any differences in private before either of you gives or refuses permission.

Now your kids must get consent from both of you. Simply say, "Dad and I will talk it over and let you know."

This allows time to think before you answer. Your children soon learn there's no point in approaching Mom or Dad individually.

Be sure to reaffirm your unity to them regularly. "Dad and I have decided . . . ." "Dad and I have talked about it, and . . . ."

Begin now.

Otherwise, get set to be outmaneuvered by an adolescent with years of experience.

---

> May the God of endurance and encouragement grant you to live in such harmony with one another, in accord with Christ Jesus. Romans 15:5

## P.S.

Kids who try all the angles are not worse than those who never question you. They're just more creative.

# Mom, the Chief Nurturer

That phrase sounds old-fashioned, perhaps outmoded.

Not necessarily.

True, many dads display tenderness and sensitivity.

Yet almost always it's Mommy who runs to kiss the boo-boo, who more likely sheds tears of joy and empathy. God wired us this way.

That's not weakness. That's strength.

At work, you may need to operate like a man. It can be a struggle to set that aside at home. You rush to keep up and sometimes think you will crack.

Heed that signal to pare down nonessentials and replenish.

Now, as in the beginning, Mom is the heart of the home. The glue that keeps everyone connected.

Your family counts on you to care. With a smile, you can set their world to rights. So you listen, although you yearn for time alone. You hug the child who just drove you to the brink of losing it.

Again.

Never discount the worth of your natural love and tenderness. They come from the Creator. As Christian moms, we can love our children because Jesus loved us all first.

You may rise to the top at work and eventually receive a gold watch or an engraved plaque.

Nice.

As a mom, you cooperate with God in shaping and rearing human beings.

Lose sight of that, and you lose who you are.

You can choose to define mothering as a burden. Or call it what it is: a privilege.

Call it joy.

---

> But the fruit of the Spirit is love, joy, peace, patience, kindness, goodness, faithfulness, gentleness, self-control; against such things there is no law.
> Galatians 5:22–23

P.S.

Can any woman live up to this list? Not on our own and not all the time. Read it again. Notice who produces the fruit, and be at peace.

# Move from Conflict to Strength

Your child arrived with a will of granite.

Few moms are ready for that.

Now confrontations fill your days. The endless tug-of-war leaves you limp.

What to do?

First, give up self-doubt. God put you in charge. You're the mom, so it's okay to act like it. Be loving but decisive. Set rules and penalties that are firm but fair.

Then make them stick. Your determination needs to be just as strong as your child's. If you cave in to coaxing, your child loses. Kids need respect for authority to function successfully in school and in life.

Stand your ground today, or get ready to start over tomorrow.

View arguing as a delay tactic. Don't respond. Instead, quietly explain your predetermined guidelines clearly and repeatedly. Within those boundaries, allow your child to make choices, which will feel like a win.

Spend your energy on what matters, like instilling clear principles of right and wrong.

Your privilege—and it won't feel like one—is to help your youngster harness this rock-hard will toward productive energy.

Self-control will grow, and so will your child. One day your young adult will be ready for big challenges.

So forget trying to turn granite into squeezable clay.

The Great Designer never makes a mistake.

---

> The Spirit of God has made me, and the breath of the Almighty gives me life. Job 33:4

## P.S.

No need to pay for a personal trainer to help you grow strong. You already have one in-house.

# So What Am I, Chopped Liver?

You didn't start out to be a stepmother. You just loved the man and married him.

He came with strings attached—his children. Now they're yours too.

You believed love would smooth out difficulties, but to them, you remain an unwelcome intruder.

Will they ever love you for you?

Probably.

Someday.

Look through their eyes. If their mother died, loving you may feel like forgetting she ever lived.

Children of divorce cling to the hope their parents will reconcile. Otherwise they cannot escape aching truth: their parents chose to separate and divorce.

Either way, grieving can last a long time. Be patient while these youngsters heal.

Love them anyway.

Be kind anyway.

Their dad feels caught in the middle, loving them and loving you.

Remind yourself and these youngsters that when you married their dad, you said yes to them too. You chose this package, and you are here to stay.

Pray for your marriage and your family, trusting Jesus Christ to bring wholeness out of brokenness.

Be at peace.

He who knows the future will use you to bless these children in ways you cannot know right now.

Count on loving imperfectly.

Just love imperfectly with all your heart.

And every morning, decide again to walk with contentment the fine line you chose.

> He has shown you, O man, what is good; And what does the LORD require of you But to do justly, To love mercy, And to walk humbly with your God?
> Micah 6:8 (NKJV)

## P.S.

Ask the Savior to create enduring bonds between you and your new family, just as in broken bones that grow stronger at the break.

# Living with Uncertainty

From the beginning we want to protect our children, yet dangers lurk all around.

Night and day, questions gnaw away at us.

*What if another student brings a gun to school?*

*What if a kidnapper snatches my daughter?*

*What if my son doesn't recover?*

The more you play out the possibilities, the nearer you come to panic. The media seeds and cultivates fear, but our anxiety traces back to eternal, indisputable truth. We are powerless. We cannot even predict what lies ahead, let alone control it.

No escape, no place of safety exists on this earth.

That reality leaves you gasping for air.

Your only antidote is the same as from the beginning. Trust the One who writes the future. Ask Him to quiet your heart and mind. Equip your inner arsenal against fear by storing up Bible verses that speak of God's protection and peace as well as Jesus' mercy and promise of salvation. When worry rises up, deliberately turn your thoughts as you would change TV channels.

To be alive is to be at risk.

To let *What ifs* camp out in your mind is a choice.

Your child is never alone.

And neither are you.

Take these Scripture verses personally, as if they were written just for you.

They were.

> My help comes from the LORD, who made heaven and earth. He will not let your foot be moved; He who keeps you will not slumber. Psalm 121:2–3

## P.S.

Bask in the Savior's loving protection, and let His peace drive out panic.

# Mealtimes Nourish Family Bonds

Trying to gather the family in one spot for meals takes too much effort.

Or does it?

Sharing a meal means sharing lives. It builds family strength and reminds everyone, "I belong here. This is my family."

That recognition nourishes emotional health and stability in each one.

After deciding which meal works best, announce a new house rule. Everyone is to show up for that meal, every day. Expect grumbles, but allow few exceptions. Your insistence signals that this matters.

Whether you're serving gourmet or takeout, begin by thanking the Giver. Take turns saying grace, and include your preschoolers. Let each one share a personal high and low of the day while the rest listen. A high may be as big as a job promotion or making the team, or as small as learning to tie one's shoe. Lows, too, may be major or minor.

No teasing allowed, even if one mumbles and another stammers.

If you miss a meal together or if someone wants to quit, don't panic. Quietly persevere. As each individual better understands the others, your family will forge closer bonds than ever before. You'll gain new insights into your kids and your husband and how to pray for them.

Wrap up with a table prayer, "popcorn prayers," or the Lord's Prayer.

Eating together brings each one back to what your family stands for.

Even when "nothing happens," something wonderful and worthwhile takes place.

Each one is reminded again: We are family. We are one.

---

> The eyes of all look to You [O Lord], and You give them their food in due season. Psalm 145:15

## P.S.

At first this may feel difficult, as your family gets comfortable with sharing, but why not try it? Before long, no one will want to miss out.

# Are Your Kids Training You to Obey?

Some kids quickly master behavioral training.
 Of their parents.
 To get what they want, they whine.
 They pout.
 They yell.
 Sometimes they hit their parents.
 What they don't do is give in.
 These youngsters know that eventually Mommy or Daddy will say, "Oh, all right. But this is the last time!

 "*Do—you—under—stand—me?*"
 Next time (and there's *always* a next time), each cast member slips into character, and the drama begins again.

 You can stop this manipulation any time you're ready. The same Lord who said "Children, obey your parents" gives you authority to set limits and quietly stand your ground.

 Expect your child to keep testing, assuming you will concede as you always have before. If you do, you will supply fresh hope to this young resistance fighter. Next time, you will be back where you started, and you'll need to begin again.

 You may feel uneasy standing firm, especially if you prefer to be more a friend than a parent.

Don't fall into that trap.

Rather, pray for new eyes to see your role more clearly and for the will to carry on.

Sometimes you will fail, as humans do. Pray for forgiveness in Christ and begin again. Pray for love that cancels out your anger and enables you to forgive your child.

Resolve again you will not budge, and draw courage from knowing your motive is love.

If you teach your kids that the world does not revolve around them, you will bless them for life.

Their teachers will thank you.

So will every other person in their lives, now and in the future.

---

For God gave us a spirit not of fear but of power and love and self-control.
2 Timothy 1:7

## P.S.

The individual who lives in a world bounded on all sides by the pronoun *I* inhabits a very small domain.

# Making Sense of the Struggle and Finding Hope

Rearing children is like taking the test before we get the textbook.

Collapsing into bed every night, too exhausted to think, let alone pray.

Wondering whether we can make it through another twenty-four hours of mothering our gifts from God.

The mom we want to be never frowns, never yells, never loses her temper.

The mom who lives in our skin does, of course. Often.

Each night you rake yourself over the same old hot coals. Every tomorrow you start over and, well, mess up again.

Peace will come when you stop comparing yourself with perfection.

Every day you live, you love and cope the best way you know how.

Be content with that.

Otherwise you will mountain-climb over molehills all your days.

When you feel stressed, pause and pray for strength. Remember that God's grace in Christ washes away sin and makes you new.

Rejoice.

Trust.

Take courage.

Your imperfect love, freely given, covers a multitude of shortcomings.

Day by day, you and your children learn and grow.

Together you write the story of your family and love that overshadows the dark.

The One who paired you together planned it that way.

---

> By this we know love, that He laid down His life for us, and we ought to lay down our lives for the brothers. . . . By this we shall know that we are of the truth and reassure our heart before Him.
> 1 John 3:16, 19

## P.S.

Be patient as the mom who lives in your skin develops into the woman God made her to be.

# Resistance Comes in Different Packages

Defiant children are easy to spot.

These kids specialize in the word *no* and comply only when faced with an immovable parent.

Some will test you several times a day, checking to see if you still mean it.

Youngsters with less taste for confrontation employ more covert strategies.

Faulty hearing.

Selective amnesia.

Laughing and turning on the charm, thereby distracting the parent.

Outwardly more agreeable kids often are no more cooperative than outright challengers. They're just easier to live with.

Be assured that none of these children are "bad." They just prefer to have it their way.

Whatever the personality of each child, make it your goal to bring out the best qualities in each one.

You're the mom, remember?

God put you in charge, so be loving but decisive.

Stick to the basics of sound parenting. Lay out limits within which your kids can make choices. This allows them to exercise some freedom and control.

Set rules and penalties that are firm but fair, then don't back down.

If today you yield, tomorrow you go back to square one.

Through it all, strive to keep your voice calm, and refuse to argue.

If you give in to coaxing, your children will lose, no matter what their intelligence, skills, or natural talents may be. No matter what your financial status is.

Home is where youngsters practice for tomorrow.

Kids who don't learn respect for authority grow up disadvantaged.

For life.

---

> Children, obey your parents in the Lord, for this is right. Ephesians 6:1

## P.S.

If being in authority feels uncomfortable, remember you need not be stern and forbidding. Just be resolute—and smile.

# Take It Easier

Watch out for enticing snares that come disguised as worthwhile goals.

It starts with an appealing theme: "Be all you can be." Moms often expand that to include "Be all a mother is supposed to be." The next logical add-on is "Raise children who are as near to perfect as humanly possible."

At first all this sounds harmless, even noble. What it does not sound like is fun.

Not for you or for your kids.

Struggle to meet those standards and you could go from dedicated to driven.

If that happens, your children will become something you *do*. Proof of your competence as a "good mother." Extensions of you, rather than individuals to love for themselves.

Some moms try so hard that they go through each day with gritted teeth. Their body language screams the message: this is serious business.

These women devour every book, watch every TV expert, and then try out each one's theory.

End this madness.

You could memorize a stack of theories but miss what matters most:

Your child, opening up and blooming before you.

Love that lights up dark days.

The wonder and joy of this small person.

God's love gift to you, wrapped in flesh and bones. On loan to you, for just a little while.

> See to it that no one takes you captive by philosophy and empty deceit, according to human tradition, according to the elemental spirits of the world, and not according to Christ. Colossians 2:8

## P.S.

Give up theories of "experts" and talking heads. Hang around Christian moms whose kids behave in ways that would make you proud. Learn from them.

# Why Bother Going to Church?

Sometimes the Sunday-morning hassle feels like too much. That weekly round of moans and groans. That little voice inside yammers, *Why bother?*

You rouse the grumblers and get everyone fed and dressed.

Finally you make it to the church and collapse into your seat. Not for the first time, you wonder, *Does any of this matter?*

Yes.

The other six days, life can seem hostile, even to your children. For many kids, school feels like torment. Teasing, ridicule, or bullying follows them around.

Friends disappoint them.

Temptations crowd in. Why not cheat and ace the test? Drugs may be readily available. Why not?

Yet when you ask, "How was your day?" you get, "Fine."

And it's not as though adults get a pass on the job.

Church offers a welcoming refuge from such everyday strains. Here, people accept you as you are and love you before they know you. Even youngsters who mess up rate smiles and hugs. Here your kids meet other Christian kids and are reminded how much Jesus loves them.

We arrive hungry, and Jesus truly comes to us in Word and Sacrament. He feeds us with the bread of life, giving us strength to live in a world of conflict and doubt.

We remember once more that Christ living within us enables us to forgive.

Once more we hear that Jesus' love empowers us to love as He loves.

Worshiping with other believers reminds us who we are.

Why go to church? Your entire family will leave feeling stronger, more able to face whatever the week may bring.

Most would say the value of these gifts far outweighs the "Sunday-morning hassle."

How about you?

> Let us hold fast the confession of our hope without wavering, for He who promised is faithful. Hebrews 10:23

## P.S.

Many parents want their kids to be free to choose as adults whether they want to go to church. Funny . . . no one ever applies that same logic to, say, brushing teeth.

# Mom, the Balance Beam Pro

Every day we moms walk a balance beam between trashing our child's hopes and over-praising.

Some of us try to protect our kids from disappointment by being "realistic." They bring us their dreams and grand schemes. We pinpoint hindrances and difficulties. They walk away with shoulders sagging, and we wonder why.

Some of us go overboard the other way. We routinely crow "You're amazing" or "That's awesome" over not very much. Then our well-intentioned words become empty applause.

Let's be truer to our mission and avoid either extreme.

Only our Creator knows what He planted in each child. That lies beyond our sight as surely as the oak tree waits within the acorn.

Obvious talents may show up early. Inherent abilities of deeper value may not appear for years.

What your kids need most is your unwavering faith. This infuses courage to experiment and sometimes fail, then try again.

What about the one who struggles, the one who baffles you or makes you bite your nails? That youngster craves your love and reassurance most of all.

Remind each child, not just your blue-ribbon kid, that he or she is uniquely and wonderfully made for a purpose. One day, each one will know what it is.

And so will you.

Be patient as you watch your children find their way and develop into themselves. Mighty oaks take awhile to grow.

So do mighty moms.

---

My son, if your heart is wise, my heart too will be glad. Proverbs 23:15

## P.S.

Youngsters who earn praise for honest effort gain self-confidence and a healthy sense of pride.

# Don't Wait Too Long to Talk about Sex

Some parents believe children remain unaware of sex until their hormones kick in.

Wrong.

Youngsters notice Mommy and Daddy's long hugs and kisses. They know there's something special going on.

Parents who never touch each other or who speak rudely send a message too.

What happens at home influences your child's perspective on sex more than The Talk you plan to give. Someday.

More than television or classroom lectures.

Students in typical sex education classes learn about body parts, birth control, and STD prevention. Usually they're told all types of sexual behavior are equally acceptable.

Morals and values? Not much.

That's where you come in.

Help your kids look through eyes of faith.

Watch TV as a family. This allows natural lead-ins to talk about sexual innuendos and behavior onscreen.

Ask your children's opinions and listen calmly to their responses. Don't panic if your responses sound awkward.

Gently stress that God intended the sexual relationship to be a unique bond between husband and wife, reserved for marriage.

Older kids will say that's not how it works in the real world.

Remind them Christians seek to live by the Bible, not the culture.

Start early so your kids integrate the Christian perspective on sex long before adolescence.

Don't worry about confusing or worrying your younger children. They'll absorb only what they're ready for.

Wouldn't you rather your kids learn the Christian view of sexuality and intercourse first?

Then now's the time. Start talking.

---

> Therefore a man shall leave his father and his mother and hold fast to his wife, and they shall become one flesh.
> Genesis 2:24

## P.S.

Your casual conversations and actions speak loudly. Your kids will note whether that echoes what you say when talking to them about sex.

# Never Underestimate Dear Old Dad

Some people consider fathers irrelevant for modern kids.

Some fathers agree and go missing. Others seem uninterested in their children.

Too bad. Kids need their imperfect dads to provide a male point of view.

That touch of reckless.

That bit of brag.

The little-boy teasing, prodding, challenging. Sounding tough.

Every mom wants to protect her children and warns, "Be careful!"

Dads say, "Go for it!"

When a child stumbles, Mom asks, "Are you okay, honey?"

Dad calls, "You can do it!"

Kids benefit from both.

These two perspectives complement each other, a concept that originated in the all-knowing, all-wise mind of our heavenly Father.

In recent years, numerous studies proved that male and female brains are wired differently. This shocked no one but the researchers. Each parent brings something unique to rearing their children.

Something precious.

Think of dads as the perfect counterpart to moms. The balance that helps children get ready for the world "out there," when Mom won't be available to rescue them.

Every boy and girl knows it's great to have a mom who loves you.

But any kid will tell you it's even better to have a mom *and* a dad who love you.

---

> So God created man in His own image, in the image of God He created him; male and female He created them.
> Genesis 1:27

## P.S.

Differences are not the same as shortcomings. Not in your kids. Not in your spouse.

# Failure Rates a Passing Grade

Some kids lug around a heavy burden they cannot shed.

They're convinced their parents expect them to shine.

Every time.

We loving moms never say those words exactly, but we drop subtle hints.

Kids seldom read them as subtle.

Perhaps one child achieves and another does not. That one struggles mightily for every small gain.

We tell ourselves we would never compare one child with another. Yet without realizing it, we do. Blame it on our need to look good to others. Letting go of that is hard.

Tack this to your mental bulletin board: God can turn a youngster's botched attempts into tools for learning and growth.

That's reason enough to keep praying.

Whatever their capabilities, your kids cannot see themselves as whole unless you do. Your unwavering acceptance of their individuality coaxes each one into bloom.

Inevitably, they will face disappointments. Be ready to hug and listen and ask what useful lessons they learned for next time. Reassure them that your love remains unchanged and that God is always on their side. Teach them that Christ's work within us makes us whole.

Be sure your children understand one basic truth of life always holds true: people who succeed at anything almost always work hard.

Tell them that's where your expectations end.

Failures equal temporary interruptions. Label them nothing more and nothing less in your family.

You will set your children free to discover who they are.

---

> Wait for the LORD; be strong, and let your heart take courage; wait for the LORD! Psalm 27:14

## P.S.

You bless your kids for life when you love them as they are—and let them know it.

# Mothering: Stretching beyond Yourself

Becoming a mother was the easy part.

It's being a mom that presents the ongoing challenge.

We knew beforehand that rearing our child would absorb us for years on end. We read all the books and dreamed all the dreams. But that was concept. Word pictures, with a bit of fantasy thrown in.

This is grueling reality.

Every mom knows the feeling of being utterly drained. Today you cannot shake it, no matter how hard you try. Your heart reminds you of the privilege, the joy of rearing your children. Your body screams, "Exhausted!"

Your spirit, too, cries out for renewal. You ache for time alone. To be pampered and indulged would be bliss. A week at a spa would transform your mood. For a while.

For lasting refreshment, turn to the same God who made you a mother. His grace in Jesus Christ covers all your failings. The Spirit of God will guide you, refuel your stamina, and replenish your joy. He who assigned your task will meet your every need.

Shift your gaze beyond this day.

You're living your most important accomplishment right now. Believe it. Rearing your children will impact more future lives than you could imagine.

They are your legacy to the world.

And your gift.

> He gives power to the weak, And to those who have no might He increases strength. Isaiah 40:29 (NKJV)

P.S.

Once you take the longer view, each day's demands seem less overwhelming. Regard them always as part of the whole.

# The Child in Your Mind May Not Be the Child in Your Life

Long before we become parents, we daydream and form mental pictures.

As our flesh-and-blood children grow, we may be in for a shock.

She's a tomboy, not a girl who loves ruffles. He'd rather draw a picture than hit a ball.

Still, old dreams die hard. So we endlessly sign up our kids for activities, hoping to spark new interests.

Sometimes there are no sparks, just a string of failures that warp their self-image.

Eventually we remember what we said we knew all along: God creates one-of-a-kinds. This youngster who grooves to a tune we can't hear is a marvel too.

Love does not design a beautiful mold, then squeeze the child into it.

Love embraces the child before us.

That's our privilege—and our wonderful/fearful challenge as moms. Sooner or later, wise moms come to understand this truth: kids who feel accepted as they are conclude that they are okay and they are loved.

Provide a sturdy framework of love and faith, and then revel in your family's individuality.

Authenticity. What you say is what you do.

Consistency. You said it yesterday and you still mean it today.

Clear limits. Ensure your kids understand, and then, within those parameters, allow choices.

Speak your love so often that they tell you to quit. (They won't mean it.)

Live out your faith in Jesus so they see its reality.

Do that, and you give your children a secure enclosure within which they find freedom to explore and figure out who they are.

So do you.

(Growth has no age limits.)

---

[Jesus said,] "You shall love your neighbor as yourself." Matthew 19:19

[Jesus said,] "So now faith, hope, and love abide, these three; but the greatest of these is love." 1 Corinthians 13:13

## P.S.

It's well not to confuse our dreams for our children with the dreams God planted within them.

# Your Pedestal Is Crumbling, But That's Okay

Maybe there was a time when you pictured a statue of you in the park with a brass plaque inscribed, "World's Best Mother." Now there are days when you feel like running away from home.

Every mom has days like that.

To borrow from that old Peace Corps slogan, motherhood always will be "the hardest job you'll ever love."

Mothering demands all you've got, and then some—day after day after wearying day.

Once you judged other moms who couldn't keep up and thought them inept. Today, it's lunchtime, and you haven't combed your hair or shed your bathrobe because the baby won't stop crying. The capper is your six-year-old's stomach flu. Worse yet, you just yelled at your innocent three-year-old.

What happened to the calm, wonderful mother you planned to be?

Face it. She lived in a world of dreams.

Say hello to the flesh-and-blood mom who is coping on the scene. Trying hard. Loving big. Messing up and making mistakes, but hanging in there.

So you're not perfect.

So what?

Thank God for this moment of truth and understanding. Today you know better than yesterday that you're only human and that's okay.

The cross of Christ covers every weakness and sets you free to be who you are.

Live your life, smile at your kids, and laugh at your inadequacies.

No apologies required, even on your bad days.

---

I can do all things through Christ who strengthens me. Philippians 4:13 (NKJV)

## P.S.

When you doubt yourself, remember that God trusted you to be the mother of your children. He knows you better than you know yourself.

# Pause and Be Refreshed

Life can get lost in the living.

We reach the end of the week and wonder where it went.

Life is full, we say; life is good. Yet we feel as empty as a riverbed in time of drought.

We arrive at this desert place any time we forget how we are made.

On that sixth day of creation, God formed human beings in His image.

On the seventh day, He rested, looked over His work, and weighed its value.

What if you set aside one quiet day a week, every week? A time to stop and remember whose you are. A time to rest and reflect on the six days just lived, and a time to receive the gifts that only Jesus can give.

Consider the many ways you lived out love.

Focus on each child by name.

Growing.

Changing.

Learning.

Name each one who loves you and needs you. Thank God for these gifts.

When failures float to the surface, lay your packets of pain at the cross. Leave them there, then drink in refreshment and renewal.

See again the meaning in what you do every day. Allow yourself to feel good about the life you are living right now.

Every week boasts moments of joy, yours to savor and replay.

Each day you leave footprints on the future. Let your heart rejoice.

---

> And God saw everything that He had made, and behold, it was very good. . . . And He rested on the seventh day from all His work that He had done. Genesis 1:31a; 2:2b

## P.S.

Our Creator infuses every human being with His rhythm of life. When we ignore that, our lives get out of sync.

# A Woman of Lasting Influence

Every other accomplishment takes second place to being a mom.

In the midst of our hurry years, we may find that hard to believe. On any day of the week, we perform juggling acts that amaze no one but ourselves.

Always a new challenge.

Always the tiredness.

Sometimes you wonder if you'll ever get your life back.

Or your joy.

You will if you look deeper. And wider.

Snatch a few minutes alone and reflect on your life in Christ. Leave what troubles you at His cross. Then focus on every reason for thanks. Rejoice in your children, each one a complex bundle of strengths and challenges.

Let truth sink in deep. Your love and cheers, your sweat and your tears are helping these youngsters grow into the individuals God created them to be.

Mark this well: You're not dithering away your time. Your mothering will live on. You are rearing somebody's parent, somebody's grandparent, leaving your mark on generations yet to be born.

Influencing tomorrows you will never see.

Every minute holds lasting value.

Day after day, you're rearing your children, growing a family, making a life. Refuse to discount your life's work.

You are a mother by God's design, redeemed by Jesus Christ, and led by His Spirit.

Each child is your child by God's design.

Live in the joy of knowing no one else can mother your kids or love your kids as well as you can. Wrap the gladness of what's good around you, and feel the warmth of it.

You are right where you are meant to be.

---

> The steadfast love of the LORD is from everlasting to everlasting on those who fear Him, and His righteousness to children's children. Psalm 103:17

## P.S.

This you can rely on: God is faithful. Your love for your children matters. Every day your kids grow stronger, and so do you. It is enough for whatever comes.

So now faith, hope, and love abide, these three; but the greatest of these is love.
1 Corinthians 13:13

*Godly Moms: Strength from the Inside Out* is Lenore Buth's fifth book, all published by Concordia. It follows *How to Speak Confidently with Your Child about Sex,* now in its fifth edition.

Lenore also co-authored a *LifeLight* Bible study and wrote numerous articles for national magazines and regional newspapers. An Illinois publication ran her monthly column for ten years. Whether she is writing or speaking to an audience, her words flow out of a lifelong faith in Jesus.

She and her husband have four daughters and eight grandchildren. After Illinois came California and then a job-related move to the Northwest. Lenore and Bob now reside in a Sacramento suburb.